Unlocking Your Purpose Journal

Danielle Johnson

Unless otherwise indicated, all scriptures quotations are taken from the Holy Bible, New Living Translation copyright 1996, 2004, 2007, 2015 by Tyndale House Foundation, Used by permission of Tyndale House Publishers, Inc., Carol Stream, Illinois, 60188. All rights reserved.

Book Cover Design: Michelle Stimpson

Printed by Prize Publishing House, LLC in the United States of America.

First printing edition 2025.

Prize Publishing House
P.O. Box 9856, Chesapeake, VA 23321
www.PrizePublishingHouse.com

ISBN (Paperback): 979-8-9925617-4-6

Beautiful words stir my heart. I will recite a lovely poem about the king, for my tongue is like the pen of a skillful poet.

Psalm 45:1

David's Prayer of Thanks
(1 Chronicles 17:16-27)

Then King David went in and sat before the LORD and prayed,

"Who am I, O LORD God, and what is my family, that you have brought me this far? 17 And now, O God, in addition to everything else, you speak of giving your servant a lasting dynasty! You speak as though I were someone very great, O LORD God!

18 "What more can I say to you about the way you have honored me? You know what your servant is really like. 19 For the sake of your servant, O LORD, and according to your will, you have done all these great things and have made them known.

20 "O LORD, there is no one like you. We have never even heard of another God like you! 21 What other nation on earth is like your people Israel? What other nation, O God, have you redeemed from slavery to be your own people? You made a great name for yourself when you redeemed your people from Egypt. You performed awesome miracles and drove out the nations that stood in their way. 22 You chose Israel to be your very own people forever, and you, O LORD, became their God.

23 "And now, O LORD, I am your servant; do as you have promised concerning me and my family. May it be a promise that will last forever. 24 And may your name be established and honored forever so that everyone will say, 'The LORD of Heaven's Armies, the God of Israel, is Israel's God!' And may the house of your servant David continue before you forever.

25 "O my God, I have been bold enough to pray to you because you have revealed to your servant that you will build a house for him—a dynasty of kings! 26 For you are God, O LORD. And you have promised these good things to your servant. 27 And now, it has pleased you to bless the house of your servant, so that it will continue forever before you. For when you grant a blessing, O LORD, it is an eternal blessing!"

May the words of my mouth and the meditation of my heart be pleasing to you, O LORD, my rock and my redeemer.

Psalm 19:14

Put me on trial, LORD, and cross-examine me. Test my motives and my heart.

Psalm 26: 2

Only ask, and I will make the nations your inheritance, the ends of the earth your possession.
Psalm 2:8

Your word is a lamp to guide my feet and a light for my path.
Psalm 119:105

Create in me a clean heart, O God. Renew a loyal spirit within me.
Psalm 51:10

But you, O LORD, are a shield around me; you are my glory, the one who holds my head high.
Psalm 3:3

I cried out to the LORD, and he answered me from his holy mountain.
Psalm 3:4

For you bless the godly, O LORD; you surround them with your shield of love.

Psalm 5:12

But I trust in your unfailing love. I will rejoice because you have rescued me.

Psalm 13:5

In peace I will lie down and sleep, for you alone, O LORD, will keep me safe.
Psalm 4:8

I have hidden your word in my heart, that I might not sin against you.
Psalm 119:11

I said to the LORD, "You are my Master! Every good thing I have comes from you."
Psalm 16:2

Seek the Kingdom of God above all else, and live righteously, and he will give you everything you need.
Matthew 6:33

Work willingly at whatever you do, as though you were working for the LORD rather than for people.
Colossians 3:23

_____

_____

_____

_____

_____

_____

_____

_____

_____

_____

_____

_____

_____

_____

_____

_____

_____

_____

_____

_____

_____

_____

_____

_____

_____

Then you will experience God's peace, which exceeds anything we can understand. His peace will guard your hearts and minds as you live in Christ Jesus.

Philippians 4:7

Listen to my voice in the morning, LORD. Each morning I bring my requests to you and wait expectantly.
Psalm 5:3

But what joy for all who take refuge in him!
Psalm 2:12

For everything there is a season, a time for every activity under heaven.

Ecclesiastes 3:1

Wait patiently for the LORD. Be brave and courageous. Yes, wait patiently for the LORD.
Psalm 27:14

May the LORD bless you and protect you. May the LORD smile on you and be gracious to you.
Numbers 6:24-25

Give thanks to the LORD, for he is good! His faithful love endures forever.
Psalm 118:1

Yet I am confident I will see the LORD's goodness while I am here in the land of the living.

Psalm 27:13

God is not a man, so he does not lie. He is not human, so he does not change his mind. Has he ever spoken and failed to act? Has he ever promised and not carried it through?
Numbers 23:19

No one will be able to stand against you as long as you live. For I will be with you as I was with Moses. I will not fail you or abandon you.

Joshua 1:5

Mark out a straight path for your feet; stay on the safe path.
Proverbs 4:26

May the LORD show you his favor and give you his peace.
Numbers 6:26

Don't get sidetracked; keep your feet from following evil.
Proverbs 4:27

Give thanks to the LORD; his faithful love endures forever!
2 Chronicles 20:21

Let the wise listen to these proverbs and become even wiser. Let those with understanding receive guidance.

Proverbs 1:5

They were calling out to each other, "Holy, holy, holy is the LORD of Heaven's Armies! The whole earth is filled with his glory."
Isaiah 6:3

"For I know the plans I have for you," says the LORD. "They are plans for good and not for disaster, to give you a future and a hope."

Jeremiah 29:11

Then the LORD said to me, "Write my answer plainly on tablets, so that a runner can carry the correct message to others."

Habakkuk 2:2

But the Holy Spirit produces this kind of fruit in our lives: love, joy, peace, patience, kindness, goodness, faithfulness, gentleness, and self-control. There is no law against these things!
Galatians 5:22-23

Each time he said, "My grace is all you need. My power works best in weakness." So now I am glad to boast about my weaknesses, so that the power of Christ can work through me.

2 Corinthians 12:9

Great is his faithfulness; his mercies begin afresh each morning.
Lamentations 3:23

The eyes of the LORD watch over those who do right, and his ears are open to their prayers.
But the LORD turns his face against those who do evil.
1 Peter 3:12

For the word of God will never fail.

Luke 1:37

The Spirit alone gives eternal life. Human effort accomplishes nothing. And the very words I have spoken to you are spirit and life.

John 6:63

The LORD is good to those who depend on him, to those who search for him.
Lamentations 3:25

But you belong to God, my dear children. You have already won a victory over those people, because the Spirit who lives in you is greater than the spirit who lives in the world.
1 John 4:4

And I am certain that God, who began the good work within you, will continue his work until it is finally finished on the day when Christ Jesus returns.

Philippians 1:6

My children, listen when your father corrects you. Pay attention and learn good judgment.
Proverbs 4:1

You will restore me to even greater honor and comfort me once again.
Psalm 71:21

So let's not get tired of doing what is good. At just the right time we will reap a harvest of blessing if we don't give up.

Galatians 6:9

I pray that from his glorious, unlimited resources he will empower you with inner strength through his Spirit.

Ephesians 3:16

Fear of the LORD is the foundation of true knowledge, but fools despise wisdom and discipline.
Proverbs 1:7

This means that anyone who belongs to Christ has become a new person. The old life is gone; a new life has begun!

2 Corinthians 5:17

Dear friend, I hope all is well with you and that you are as healthy in body as you are strong in spirit.
3 John 1:2

If we claim we have not sinned, we are calling God a liar and showing that his word has no place in our hearts.

1 John 1:10

But they delight in the law of the LORD, meditating on it day and night.
Psalm 1:2

May God give you more and more mercy, peace, and love.

Jude 1:2

So be truly glad. There is wonderful joy ahead, even though you must endure many trials for a little while.

1 Peter 1:6

The LORD is good, a strong refuge when trouble comes. He is close to those who trust in him.

Nahum 1:7

As the Scriptures tells us, "Anyone who trusts in him will never be disgraced."
Romans 10:11

And God never said to any of the angels, "Sit in the place of honor at my right hand until I humble your enemies, making them a footstool under your feet."
Hebrews 1:13

Trust in the LORD and do good. Then you will live safely in the land and prosper.
Psalm 37:3

Commit everything you do to the LORD. Trust him, and he will help you.
Psalm 37:5

I tell you the truth, whatever you forbid on earth will be forbidden in heaven, and whatever you permit on earth will be permitted in heaven.

Matthew 18:18

And you will know the truth, and the truth will set you free.

John 8:32

For we are not fighting against flesh-and-blood enemies, but against evil rulers and authorities of the unseen world, against mighty powers in this dark world, and against evil spirits in the heavenly places.

Ephesians 6:12

Jesus replied, "You must love the LORD your God with all your heart, all your soul, and all your mind."

Matthew 22:37

The lowly will possess the land and will live in peace and prosperity.
Psalm 37:11

For God is Spirit, so those who worship him must worship in spirit and in truth.

John 4:24

_____

_____

_____

_____

_____

_____

_____

_____

_____

_____

_____

_____

_____

_____

_____

_____

_____

_____

_____

_____

_____

_____

_____

_____

_____

_____

*But Jesus told him, "No! The Scripture say, People do not live by bread alone, but by every word
that comes from the mouth of God."*
Matthew 4:4

So God created human beings in his own image. In the image of God he created them; male and female he created them.

Genesis 1:27

Take delight in the LORD, and he will give you your heart's desires.
Psalm 37:4

For whoever finds me finds life and receives favor from the LORD.
Proverbs 8:35

The blessing of the LORD makes a person rich, and he adds no sorrow with it.
Proverbs 10:22

Those who trust in the LORD are as secure as Mount Zion; they will not be defeated but will endure forever.

Psalm 125:1

Yes, the LORD has done amazing things for us! What Joy!
Psalm 126:3

The generous will prosper; those who refresh others will themselves be refreshed.

Proverbs 11:25

The LORD is my shepherd; I have all that I need.
Psalm 23:1

He renews my strength. He guides me along right paths, bringing honor to his name.
Psalm 23:3

You will succeed in whatever you choose to do, and light will shine on the road ahead of you.
Job 22:28

It is the same with my word. I send it out, and it always produces fruit. It will accomplish all I want it to, and it will prosper everywhere I send it.

Isaiah 55:11

I tremble in fear of you; I stand in awe of your regulations.
Psalm 119:120

For the word of God is alive and powerful. It is sharper than the sharpest two-edged sword, cutting between soul and spirit, between joint and marrow. It exposes our innermost thoughts and desires.
Hebrews 4:12

_____

_____

_____

_____

_____

_____

_____

_____

_____

_____

_____

_____

_____

_____

_____

_____

_____

_____

_____

_____

_____

_____

_____

_____

_____

_____

He was the one who prayed to the God of Israel, "Oh, that you would bless me and expand my territory! Please be with me in all that I do, and keep me from all trouble and pain!" And God granted him his request.
1 Chronicles 4:10

Be still in the presence of the LORD and wait patiently for him to act. Don't worry about evil people who prosper or fret about their wicked schemes.

Psalm 37:7

Don't worry about anything; instead, pray about everything. Tell God what you need, and thank him for all he has done.

Philippians 4:6

For God has not given us a spirit of fear and timidity, but of power, love, and self-discipline.

2 Timothy 1:7

The thief's purpose is to steal and kill and destroy. My purpose is to give them a rich and satisfying life.

John 10:10

Whatever is good and perfect is a gift coming down to us from God our Father, who created all the lights in the heavens. He never changes or casts a shifting shadow.

James 1:17

Charm is deceptive, and beauty does not last; but a woman who fears the LORD will be greatly praised.
Proverbs 31:30

I will praise the LORD at all times. I will constantly speak his praises.
Psalm 34:1

Declare me innocent, O LORD, for I have acted with integrity; I have trusted in the LORD without wavering.

Psalm 26:1

Reward her for all she has done. Let her deeds publicly declare her praise.
Proverbs 31:31

I will boast only in the LORD; let all who are helpless take heart.
Psalm 34:2

But I say, love your enemies! Pray for those who persecute you!
Matthew 5:44

God blesses those who are persecuted for doing right, for the Kingdom of Heaven is theirs.

Matthew 5:10

Then the way you live will always honor and please the LORD, and your lives will produce every kind of good fruit. All the while, you will grow as you learn to know God better and better.

Colossians 1:10

So humble yourselves before God. Resist the devil, and he will flee from you.
James 4:7

No one is holy like the LORD / There is no one besides you; there is no Rock like our God.
1 Samuel 2:2

God uses it to prepare and equip his people to do every good work.
2 Timothy 3:17

For I am about to do something new. See, I have already begun! Do you not see it? I will make a pathway through the wilderness. I will create rivers in the dry wasteland.

Isaiah 43:19

Guard your heart above all else, for it determines the course of your life.
Proverbs 4:23

"Does not my word burn like fire?" says the LORD. *"Is it not like a mighty hammer that smashes a rock to pieces?*
Jeremiah 23:29

I have swept away your sins like a cloud. I have scattered your offenses like the morning mist. Oh, return to me, for I have paid the price to set you free.

Isaiah 44:22

He has removed our sins as far from us as the east is from the west.
Psalm 103:12

He is so rich in kindness and grace that he purchased our freedom with the blood of his Son and forgave our sins.
Ephesians 1:7

So now there is no condemnation for those who belong to Christ Jesus.
Romans 8:1

Take control of what I say, O LORD, and guard my lips.
Psalm 141:3

This I declare about the LORD: He alone is my refuge, my place of safety; he is my God, and I trust him.

Psalm 91:2

The LORD is merciful and compassionate, slow to get angry and filled with unfailing love.
Psalm 145:8

But you are not like that, for you are a chosen people. You are royal priests, a holy nation, God's very own possession. As a result, you can show others the goodness of God, for he called you out of the darkness into his wonderful light.

1 Peter 2:9

You must have the same attitude that Christ Jesus had.

Philippians 2:5

From eternity to eternity I am God. No one can snatch anyone out of my hand. No one can undo what I have done.

Isaiah 43:13

For I will pour out water to quench your thirst and to irrigate your parched fields. And I will pour out my Spirit on your descendants, and my blessing on your children.
Isaiah 44:3

Let the praises of God be in their mouths, and a sharp sword in their hands.

Psalm 149:6

The one thing I ask of the LORD – the thing I seek most– is to live in the house of the LORD all the days of my life, delighting in the LORD's perfections and meditating in his Temple.
Psalm 27:4

_____

_____

_____

_____

_____

_____

_____

_____

_____

_____

_____

_____

_____

_____

_____

_____

_____

_____

_____

_____

_____

_____

_____

_____

_____

_____

_____

O my Strength, to you I sing praises, for you, O God, are my refuge, the God who shows me unfailing love.
Psalm 59:17

_____
_____
_____
_____
_____
_____
_____
_____
_____
_____
_____
_____
_____
_____
_____
_____
_____
_____
_____
_____
_____
_____
_____
_____
_____
_____

From the ends of the earth, I cry to you for help when my heart is overwhelmed. Lead me to the towering rock of safety.
Psalm 61:2

For his Spirit joins with our spirit to affirm that we are God's children.
Romans 8:16

I come to you for protection, O LORD my God. Save me from my persecutors—rescue me!
Psalm 7:1

You gave them charge of everything you made, putting all things under their authority.
Psalm 8:6

_____

_____

_____

_____

_____

_____

_____

_____

_____

_____

_____

_____

_____

_____

_____

_____

_____

_____

_____

_____

_____

_____

_____

_____

_____

Now I stand on solid ground, and I will publicly praise the LORD.
Psalm 26:12

The godly will rejoice in the LORD and find shelter in him. And those who do what is right will praise him.
Psalm 64:10

_____
_____
_____
_____
_____
_____
_____
_____
_____
_____
_____
_____
_____
_____
_____
_____
_____
_____
_____
_____
_____
_____
_____
_____
_____
_____
_____

O God, you are my God; I earnestly search for you. My soul thirsts for you; my whole body longs for you in this parched and weary land where there is no water.

Psalm 63:1

He heals the brokenhearted and bandages their wounds.

Psalm 147:3

Teach me your decrees, O LORD; I will keep them to the end.
Psalm 119:33

For you are my safe refuge, a fortress where my enemies cannot reach me.
Psalm 61:3

I will exalt you, my God and King and praise your name forever and ever.
Psalm 145:1

He alone is my rock and my salvation, my fortress where I will never be shaken.
Psalm 62:2

Let every created thing give praise to the LORD, for he issued his command, and they came into being.
Psalm 148:5

He made heaven and earth, the sea, and everything in them. He keeps every promise forever.
Psalm 146:6

Praise the LORD! Sing to the LORD a new song. Sing his praises in the assembly of his faithful.
Psalm 149:1

I wait quietly before God, for my victory comes from him.
Psalm 62:1

He lets me rest in green meadows; he leads me beside peaceful streams.
Psalm 23:2

O LORD, our LORD, your majestic name fills the earth!
Psalm 8:9

But the needy will not be ignored forever; the hopes of the poor will not always be crushed.
Psalm 9:18

For the righteous LORD loves justice. The virtuous will see his face.

Psalm 11:7

He will judge the world with justice and rule the nations with fairness.
Psalm 9:8

Let each generation tell its children of your mighty acts; let them proclaim your power.
Psalm 145:4

Send out your light and your truth; let them guide me. Let them lead me to your holy mountain, to the place where you live.

Psalm 43:3

He cared for them with a true heart and led them with skillful hands.

Psalm 78:72

And we are confident that he hears us whenever we ask for anything that pleases him.
1 John 5:14

And since we know he hears us when we make our requests, we also know that he will give us what we ask for.

1 John 5:15

Taste and see that the LORD is good. Oh, the joys of those who take refuge in him!
Psalm 34:8

Surely your goodness and unfailing love will pursue me all the days of my life, and I will live in the house of the LORD forever.
Psalm 23:6

_____
_____
_____
_____
_____
_____
_____
_____
_____
_____
_____
_____
_____
_____
_____
_____
_____
_____
_____
_____
_____
_____
_____
_____
_____
_____

I pray that God, the source of hope, will fill you completely with joy and peace because you trust in him.
Then you will overflow with confident hope through the power of the Holy Spirit.
Romans 15:13

Those who trust their own insight are foolish, but anyone who walks in wisdom is safe.
Proverbs 28:26

Dear brothers and sisters, when troubles of any kind come your way, consider it an opportunity for great joy.
James 1:2

Purify me from my sins, and I will be clean; wash me, and I will be whiter than snow.
Psalm 51:7

For you know that when your faith is tested, your endurance has chance to grow.

James 1:3

So let it grow, for when your endurance is fully developed, you will be perfect and complete,
needing nothing.
James 1:4

Shout with joy to the LORD, all the earth!
Psalm 100:1

There is no greater love than to lay down one's life for one's friends.
John 15:13

_____

_____

_____

_____

_____

_____

_____

_____

_____

_____

_____

_____

_____

_____

_____

_____

_____

_____

_____

_____

_____

_____

_____

_____

_____

_____

Jesus told him, "I am the way, the truth, and the life. No one can come to the Father except through me."
John 14:6

Even if that person wrongs you seven times a day and each time turns again and asks forgiveness, you must forgive.

Luke 17:4

When we were utterly helpless, Christ came at just the right time and died for us sinners.
Romans 5:6

For I decided that while I was with you I would forget everything except Jesus Christ, the one who was crucified.

1 Corinthians 2:2

_____
_____
_____
_____
_____
_____
_____
_____
_____
_____
_____
_____
_____
_____
_____
_____
_____
_____
_____
_____
_____
_____
_____
_____
_____
_____
_____
_____
_____
_____

"I will firmly plant them there in their own land. They will never again be uprooted from the land I have given them," says the LORD your God.
Amos 9:15

Sing, O heavens, for the LORD has done this wondrous thing. Shout for joy, O depths of the earth!
Break into song.
Isaiah 44:23

Some nations boast of their chariots and horses, but we boast in the name of the LORD our God.
Psalm 20:7

Dear children, let's not merely say that we love each other; let us show the truth by our actions.

1 John 3:18

Honor the LORD with your wealth and with the best part of everything you produce.
Proverbs 3:9

Then if my people who are called by my name will humble themselves and pray and seek my face and turn from their wicked ways, I will hear from heaven and will forgive their sins and restore their land.

2 Chronicles 7:14

_____

_____

_____

_____

_____

_____

_____

_____

_____

_____

_____

_____

_____

_____

_____

_____

_____

_____

_____

_____

_____

_____

_____

_____

_____

_____

_____

The heartfelt counsel of a friend is a sweet as perfume and incense.
Proverbs 27:9

You will keep in perfect peace all who trust in you, all whose thoughts are fixed on you!
Isaiah 26:3

So the LORD must wait for you to come to him so he can show you his love and compassion. For the
LORD is a faithful God. Blessed are those who wait for his help.

Isaiah 30:18

I am counting on the LORD; yes, I am counting on him. I have put my hope in his word.
Psalm 130:5

But those who trust in the LORD will find new strength. They will soar high on wings like eagles.
They will run and not grow weary. They will walk and not faint.
Isaiah 40:31

_____

_____

_____

_____

_____

_____

_____

_____

_____

_____

_____

_____

_____

_____

_____

_____

_____

_____

_____

_____

_____

_____

_____

_____

_____

For the LORD is your security. He will keep your foot from being caught in a trap.
Proverbs 3:26

But I will send you the Advocate—the Spirit of truth. He will come to you from the Father and will testify all about me.

John 15:26

She is energetic and strong, a hard worker.
Proverbs 31:17

A friend is always loyal, and a brother is born to help in time of need.
Proverbs 17:17

For my yoke is easy to bear, and the burden I give you is light.
Matthew 11:30

Give all your worries and cares to God, for he cares about you.
1 Peter 5:7

Don't be afraid, for I am with you. Don't be discouraged, for I am your God. I will strengthen you and help you. I will hold you up with my victorious right hand.

Isaiah 41:10

_____

_____

_____

_____

_____

_____

_____

_____

_____

_____

_____

_____

_____

_____

_____

_____

_____

_____

_____

_____

_____

_____

_____

_____

_____

_____

_____

Elijah was as human as we are, and yet when he prayed earnestly that no rain would fall, none fell for three and a half years!
James 5:17

I pray that God, the source of hope, will fill you completely with joy and peace because you trust in him. Then you will overflow with confident hope through the power of the Holy Spirit.

Romans 15:13

Devote yourselves to prayer with an alert mind and a thankful heart.

Colossians 4:2

But when I am afraid, I will put my trust in you.
Psalm 56:3

Faith shows the reality of what we hope for; it is the evidence of things we cannot see.

Hebrew 11:1

We destroy every proud obstacle that keeps people from knowing God. We capture their rebellious thoughts and teach them to obey Christ.
2 Corinthians 10:5

_____

_____

_____

_____

_____

_____

_____

_____

_____

_____

_____

_____

_____

_____

_____

_____

_____

_____

_____

_____

_____

_____

_____

_____

Dear children, let's not merely say that we love each other; let us show the truth by our actions.

1 John 3:18

But if we confess our sins to him, he is faithful and just to forgive us our sins and to cleanse us from all wickedness.

1 John 1:9

If someone claims, "I know God," but doesn't obey God's commandments, that person is a liar and is not living in the truth.

1 John 2:4

Do not love this world nor the things it offers you, for when you love the world, you do not have the love of the Father in you.
1 John 2:15

I tell you the truth, anyone who believes has eternal life.
John 6:47

Anyone who eats the bread from heaven, however, will never die.

John 6:50

Remain in me, and I will remain in you. For a branch cannot produce fruit if it is severed from the vine, and you cannot be fruitful unless you remain in me.

John 15:4

For you have given him authority over everyone. He gives eternal life to each one you have given him.
John 17:2

My prayer is not for the world, but for those you have given me, because they belong to you.
John 17:9

I'm not asking you to take them out of the world, but to keep them safe from the evil one.

John 17:15

God's will is for you to be holy, so stay away from all sexual sin.
1 Thessalonians 4:3

God has called us to live holy lives, not impure lives.
1 Thessalonians 4:7

Make it your goal to live a quiet life, minding your own business and working with your hands, just as we instructed you before.

1 Thessalonians 4:11

So be on your guard, not asleep like the others. Stay alert and be clearheaded.
1 Thessalonians 5:6

Be thankful in all circumstances, for this is God's will for you who belong to Christ Jesus.
1 Thessalonians 5:18

Do not stifle the Holy Spirit. Stay away from every kind of evil.
1 Thessalonians 5:19,22

For we are God's masterpiece. He has created us anew in Christ Jesus, so we can do the good things
he planned for us long ago.
Ephesians 2:10

Worthy

Imperfections. Empowered.
Every minute, every hour...
She sees and instinctively knows,
what is required.
She must touch the moon,
in order to not let the ways of the world
devour her heart and spirit.
A treasure, that should be kept safe.
To them, a precious artifact,
To us, that should not be put on display.
She needs a safe space.
Sister, take your foot off the brake?
That is like taking the gun off safe
Tea, coffee...
Culture is what they are after.
Rob them of their sense of security
The idea that you are better, greater...umm...
Know she is worthy!
Such a melody.
Going to...
Glowing through her tribulations.
Gold, silver...a sacred stone.
Blue Diamond, Painite, Jadeite
Her worth cannot be measured.
She is a meteorite.
Beyond price.
Oh so Valuable.

Poem written by Tamara Hamilton

About The Author

Danielle Johnson is a mom. Her favorite scripture is Jeremiah 29:11. She graduated from Tidewater Community College in 2013 with her Associates of Applied Science Degree in Management. She will be graduating in May 2023 from Regent University with her Bachelor's Degree in Professional Studies with a concentration in Teacher Education.

She has written two children's books titled Chubb the Chipmunk and Ashley Nalayla goes to the Nail Salon. She is a featured author in an anthology titled Love Hope Faith. As an author, her goal is to minister to as many readers as possible through her writing. Her desire is for readers to feel the authenticity of her story while making a difference in their lives. She hopes that the words she shares on each page reaches their hearts and are not looked at as mere words on paper, but that they feel her heart beat through her words.

Danielle's desire is for her readers to be able to see themselves in the text, and prayerfully through the Holy Spirit, be delivered and set free. Her mission to accomplish her desires with reaching her readers is through being transparent, realistic and relatable. She wants to use her testimony as a platform to minister and help women who are broken in their spirit.

For I know the plans I have for you," says the Lord. "They are plans for good and not for disaster, to give you a future and a hope. Jeremiah 29:11

www.ingramcontent.com/pod-product-compliance
Lightning Source LLC
Chambersburg PA
CBHW071736120626
46550CB00002B/542